HAL•LEONARD INSTRUMENTAL PLAY-ALONG

AUDIO ACCESS INCLUDED

Songs from **Frozen, Tangled and Enchanted**

CONTENTS

To access audio visit:
www.halleonard.com/mylibrary

Enter Code
2849-0007-2803-6189

Audio Arrangements by Peter Deneff

ISBN 978-1-4803-8721-8

Disney characters and artwork © Disney Enterprises, Inc.

WALT DISNEY MUSIC COMPANY
WONDERLAND MUSIC COMPANY, INC.

DISTRIBUTED BY

HAL•LEONARD®
CORPORATION

7777 W. BLUEMOUND RD. P.O. BOX 13819 MILWAUKEE, WI 53213

In Australia Contact:
Hal Leonard Australia Pty. Ltd.
4 Lentara Court
Cheltenham, Victoria, 3192 Australia
Email: ausadmin@halleonard.com.au

Visit Hal Leonard Online at
www.halleonard.com

DO YOU WANT TO BUILD A SNOWMAN?

from Disney's Animated Feature FROZEN

Flute

Music and Lyrics by KRISTEN ANDERSON-LOPEZ
and ROBERT LOPEZ

FOR THE FIRST TIME IN FOREVER

from Disney's Animated Feature FROZEN

Flute

Music and Lyrics by KRISTEN ANDERSON-LOPEZ
and ROBERT LOPEZ

HAPPY WORKING SONG

from Walt Disneys Pictures' ENCHANTED

Music by ALAN MENKEN
Lyrics by STEPHEN SCHWARTZ

Flute

I SEE THE LIGHT
from Walt Disney Pictures' TANGLED

Flute

Music by ALAN MENKEN
Lyrics by GLENN SLATER

poco rit.   *a tempo*

rit.   **mp**

I'VE GOT A DREAM

from Walt Disney Pictures' TANGLED

FLUTE

Music by ALAN MENKEN
Lyrics by GLENN SLATER

IN SUMMER
from Disney's Animated Feature FROZEN

Flute

Music and Lyrics by KRISTEN ANDERSON-LOPEZ
and ROBERT LOPEZ

LET IT GO

from Disney's Animated Feature FROZEN

Flute

Moderately

Music and Lyrics by KRISTEN ANDERSON-LOPEZ
and ROBERT LOPEZ

LOVE IS AN OPEN DOOR

from Disney's Animated Feature FROZEN

Flute

Music and Lyrics by KRISTEN ANDERSON-LOPEZ
and ROBERT LOPEZ

MOTHER KNOWS BEST

from Walt Disney Pictures' TANGLED

Music by ALAN MENKEN
Lyrics by GLENN SLATER

Flute

SO CLOSE

from Walt Disney Pictures' ENCHANTED

Music by ALAN MENKEN
Lyrics by STEPHEN SCHWARTZ

Flute

Moderately, with feeling

THAT'S HOW YOU KNOW

from Walt Disney Pictures' ENCHANTED

Flute

Music by ALAN MENKEN
Lyrics by STEPHEN SCHWARTZ

TRUE LOVE'S KISS

from Walt Disney Pictures' ENCHANTED

Flute

Music by ALAN MENKEN
Lyrics by STEPHEN SCHWARTZ

WHEN WILL MY LIFE BEGIN

from Walt Disney Pictures' TANGLED

Flute

Music by ALAN MENKEN
Lyrics by GLENN SLATER